# Witch Haunts

by Heidi E.Y. Stemple

Consultant: Paul F. Johnston, PhD
Historian
Washington, DC

BEARPORT
PUBLISHING

New York, New York

## Credits

Cover and Title Page, © Peter Waters/Shutterstock, © Captblack76/Shutterstock, © Matt Gibson/ Shutterstock, © Eric Isselee/Shutterstock, and © Slavko Sereda/Shutterstock; 4–5, Kim Jones; 6, © Jay Lesnansky; 7T, © Swapan Photography/Shutterstock; 7B, © 3d Pictures/Shutterstock; 8, © Jan Butchofsky/Alamy; 9T, © elnavegante/Shutterstock; 9C, © berczy04/Shutterstock; 9B, © North Wind Picture Archives/Alamy; 10, © littleny/Shutterstock; 10R, © imageBROKER/ Alamy; 11L, © Alex Malikov/Shutterstock; 11R, © Corbis; 12, © age fotostock/Alamy; 13L, © rudall30/Shutterstock; 13R, © ajt/Shutterstock; 14, © Agencja Fotograficzna Caro/Alamy; 15T, © Christin Lola/Shutterstock; 15B, © geoffrey wiggins/Shutterstock; 16, © Globuss Images/ Alamy; 17T, © Philip Mould Ltd, London/Bridgeman Images; 17B, © Mary Evans Picture Library/ Alamy; 18, © User:Chrkl/Wikimedia Commons/CC-BY-SA-3.0; 19T, © Mary Evans Picture Library/ Alamy; 19B, © The Daniel Heighton Travel Photography Collection/Alamy; 20, © Dave Kelly/Keltek Trust; 21T, © Heritage Image Partnership Ltd/Alamy; 21B, © CURAphotography/Shutterstock; 22, © Wayne Hsieh; 23T, © Kirill Vorobyev/Shutterstock; 23B, © Www78/Wikimedia Commons/ CC-BY-SA-3.0; 24, © Stephen Finn/Alamy; 25T, © Lebrecht Music and Arts Photo Library/Alamy; 25B, © Vaclav Kostal/Shutterstock; 26, © AXEL TAPIA/NOTIMEX/Newscom; 27T, © Alan Uster/ Shutterstock; 27B, © Imagemore Co., Ltd./Corbis; 31, © beeboys/Shutterstock; 32, © FotAle/ Shutterstock.

Publisher: Kenn Goin
Editor: Jessica Rudolph
Creative Director: Spencer Brinker
Design: Dawn Beard Creative
Cover: Kim Jones
Photo Researcher: Picture Perfect Professionals, LLC

*Library of Congress Cataloging-in-Publication Data*

Names: Stemple, Heidi E. Y.
Title: Witch haunts / by Heidi E.Y. Stemple.
Description: New York, New York : Bearport Publishing Company, 2017. |
    Series: Scary places series | Includes bibliographical references and
    index.
Identifiers: LCCN 2016020322 (print) | LCCN 2016022892 (ebook) | ISBN
    9781944102395 (library binding) | ISBN 9781944997397 (ebook)
Subjects: LCSH: Haunted places—Juvenile literature. | Ghosts—Juvenile
    literature. | Witches—Juvenile literature.
Classification: LCC BF1461 .S8355 2017 (print) | LCC BF1461 (ebook) | DDC
    133.4/3—dc23
LC record available at https://lccn.loc.gov/2016020322

For more information, write to Bearport Publishing Company, Inc., 45 West 21st Street, Suite 3B, New York, New York 10010. Printed in the United States of America.

10 9 8 7 6 5 4 3 2 1

# Contents

# Witch Haunts

Cauldrons, broomsticks, spells, and black cats are some of the things that witches bring to mind. Yet, stories about witches are more than just spooky **legends**. Throughout history, whenever there have been strange occurrences, people have often suspected **witchcraft**. If someone was found guilty of practicing witchcraft, the result could be a terrible death.

In this book, you will visit 11 of the spookiest witch haunts in the world. Among them are a castle haunted by the ghost of a woman suspected of being a witch, a town where many supposed witches were brutally **tortured**, and a tower where people gather on Halloween to call upon witches. As you explore each of these strange places, you can decide for yourself whether a real witch lurks there!

# The Dead Man's Curse

## Joshua Ward House, Salem, Massachusetts

In the town of Salem, there stands a three-story brick house. From the outside, the building looks ordinary. Inside, however, the ghost of a sheriff who did terrible things to accused witches is thought to linger.

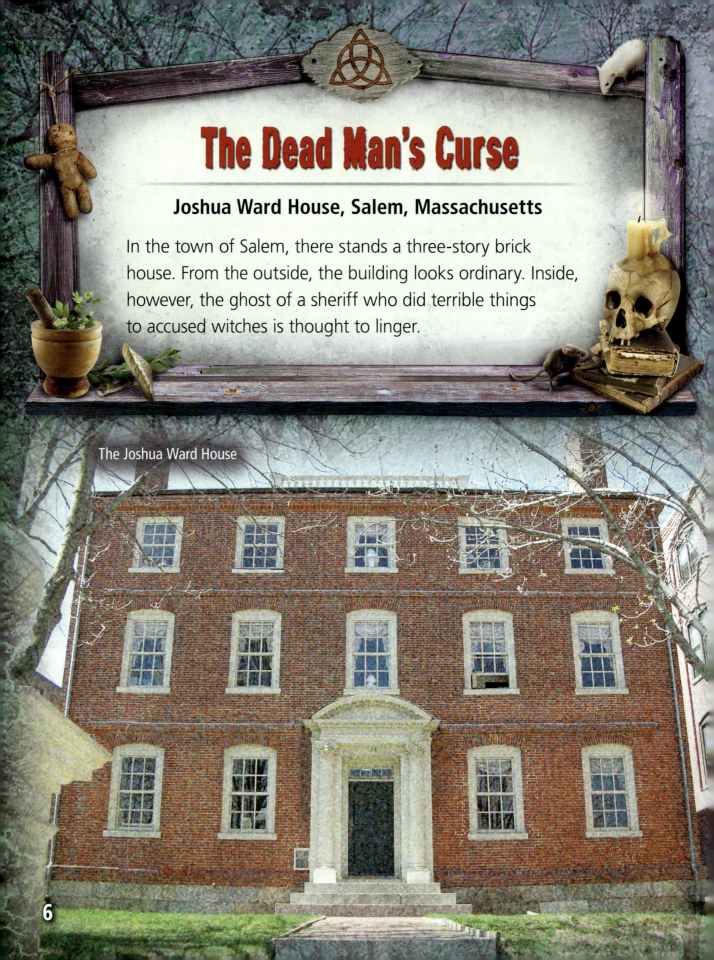

The Joshua Ward House

In 1692, something strange happened in Salem. Several girls started having frightening screaming fits. The girls were suspected of having been **bewitched**, and hundreds of innocent townspeople were accused of being witches. Sheriff George Corwin, nicknamed "the Strangler," tortured the accused by stringing them up by their necks and ankles until blood came out of their noses.

In all, 20 people were found guilty of witchcraft. Sheriff Corwin hanged most of the accused. One man shouted a **curse** at the Strangler just before he was **executed**: "Damn you! I curse you and Salem!" Soon after, Sheriff Corwin died of a heart attack when he was just 30 years old.

The sheriff's family buried him in the basement of the family's home. Almost 100 years later, a man named Joshua Ward tore down the home and built a larger house on the same spot. Some believe the **spirit** of the sheriff still lives there today. Many visitors have seen a ghostly figure sitting by the fireplace. Could it be the Strangler?

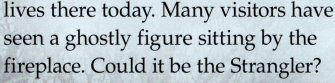

Many odd things have happened in the Joshua Ward House. Candles have jumped out of their holders, and visitors have reported being choked by invisible hands.

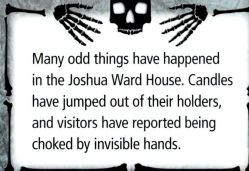

# A Deadly Witch

## Rose Hall, St. James, Jamaica

There's a legend in Jamaica surrounding a large white mansion called Rose Hall. It is said that the woman who lived there in the early 1800s was extremely cruel and **terrorized** everyone around her. The terror didn't end with her death, though. Some say the woman—called the White Witch— still resides in Rose Hall.

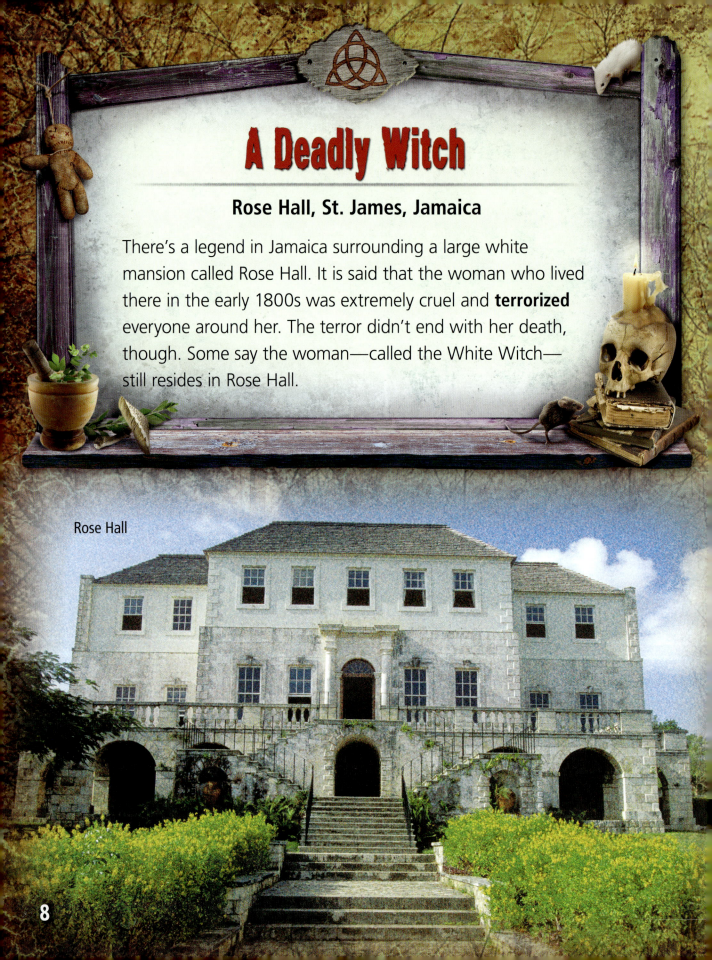

Rose Hall

When Annie Palmer married a rich plantation owner and moved into his grand house, she became widely known for the terrible treatment of the slaves who worked on his farm. Annie enjoyed watching from her balcony as the slaves were beaten. To prevent them from escaping, she had huge bear traps placed around the property. The pain of being caught in one of the traps was agonizing.

Annie wasn't just cruel. She was also deadly. She killed her first husband by poisoning his coffee. Then she murdered her next two husbands and many of her slaves. One day, a group of slaves who feared becoming Annie's next victims snuck up on her as she slept and strangled her.

Annie's body was buried on the plantation, and the slaves performed a **voodoo** ceremony to keep her spirit trapped underground. However, many people believe her spirit managed to escape. Today, some visitors to the plantation report seeing Annie's ghost. They say the White Witch rides on a horse in the fields, searching for runaway slaves, or stands on the balcony overlooking the grounds.

Slaves working on a plantation

Some tourists have claimed to see Annie's face in pictures they've taken while visiting Rose Hall.

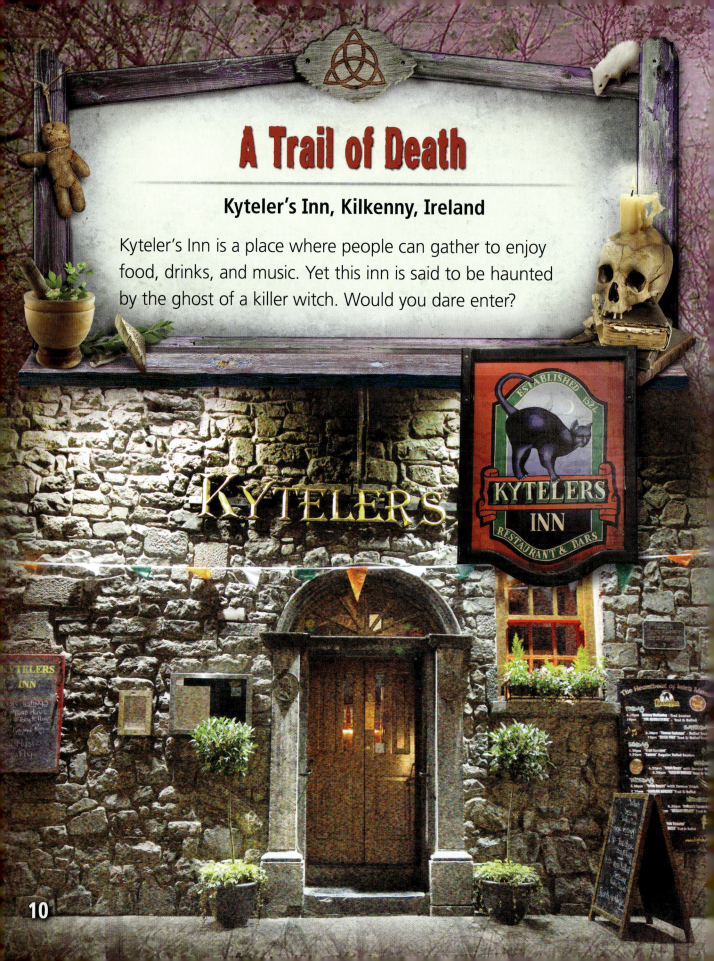

# A Trail of Death

## Kyteler's Inn, Kilkenny, Ireland

Kyteler's Inn is a place where people can gather to enjoy food, drinks, and music. Yet this inn is said to be haunted by the ghost of a killer witch. Would you dare enter?

In the early 1300s, an innkeeper named Alice Kyteler had already buried three husbands when her fourth husband, Sir John de Poer, became ill. First his hair and nails fell out, and then he grew weaker and weaker. After Sir John died, his family accused Alice of being a witch and killing him. Local church leaders put Alice on **trial** and found her guilty of witchcraft. However, just before she was to be executed, she managed to escape and flee to England.

Church leaders were determined to punish someone for the murder. They arrested Alice's maid and whipped her until she confessed that both she and Alice were witches. Soon after, the innocent maid was burned at the **stake**. Alice was never heard from again—at least not while she was alive.

Today, some people who visit and work at Kyteler's Inn say Alice has returned as a ghost. They claim to feel her presence and see her spirit. Alice's ghost, which is said to look like a dark shadow in human form, has been seen climbing the inn's stairway.

After Alice was accused of witchcraft, some of the townspeople searched her house. They claimed to have found ingredients for **potions**, including fingernails and toenails taken from **corpses**.

Accused witches being burned at the stake

# Witches Castle

## Moosham Castle, Unternberg, Austria

Moosham Castle is extremely old and has earned the nickname "Witches Castle." Why? Long ago, a judge who worked at the castle had one very important job—to rid the countryside of witches.

Moosham Castle

In the late 1600s, many Austrian villagers feared that witches were living among them. Neighbors and family members accused each other of witchcraft. Even children as young as ten years old were suspected.

Between 1675 and 1690, thousands of accused witches were imprisoned in the **dungeon** of Moosham Castle. Jailers tortured some prisoners by cutting off their hands and **branding** them with hot irons. The judge at the castle found more than 100 people guilty of witchcraft and sentenced them to death. Some were burned alive, while others were **beheaded** with an ax.

The innocent people who died at Moosham are said to walk the castle's dreary hallways. Castle visitors and staff say they get the sense that they are being watched. They tell stories about feeling ghostly fingers in their hair. Some have even felt the hot air of someone breathing down their neck, but when they turn around, no one is there.

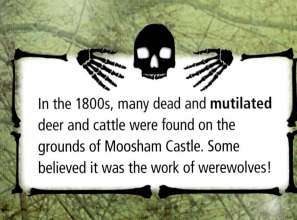

In the 1800s, many dead and **mutilated** deer and cattle were found on the grounds of Moosham Castle. Some believed it was the work of werewolves!

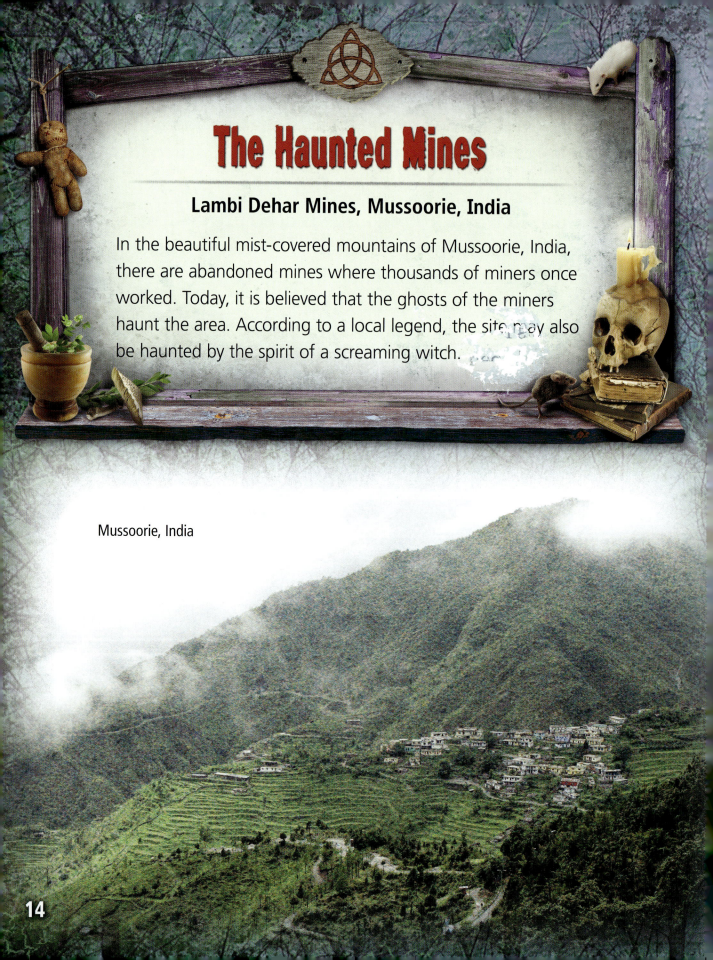

# The Haunted Mines

### Lambi Dehar Mines, Mussoorie, India

In the beautiful mist-covered mountains of Mussoorie, India, there are abandoned mines where thousands of miners once worked. Today, it is believed that the ghosts of the miners haunt the area. According to a local legend, the site may also be haunted by the spirit of a screaming witch.

Mussoorie, India

In the late 1900s, thousands of men worked day and night in the Lambi Dehar Mines, digging **limestone** from the earth. Many fell ill from breathing in the dusty air inside the mines. The workers suffered terribly, coughing up mouthfuls of blood before they finally died. When the mines were shut down in 1996, the ghosts of thousands of dead miners stayed behind. Their wails of suffering are said to still be heard.

The ghosts may not be alone, though. Many local people believe a story about the wife of one of the miners who got into an argument with her husband. In her sorrowful state, she wandered to a cliff near the mines and jumped to her death. Many say that, in death, this woman became a witch. It's thought that her screams of grief can be heard as she roams the hills and the mines. Some residents of nearby towns say the witch is even responsible for accidents that have occurred on roads close to the mines.

Many buses and trucks have slid off the cliff-side roads in Mussoorie. There was even a helicopter crash near the mines that killed almost everyone on board.

# The Gray Lady

## Glamis Castle, Angus, Scotland

Glamis Castle is surrounded by peaceful woods and beautiful gardens. It may be hard to believe that the building is the home of an unhappy spirit. In the early 1500s, one of the castle's residents, Lady Janet Douglas, was falsely accused of being a witch. Today, her spirit—known as the Gray Lady— wanders Glamis Castle, unable to find peace.

Glamis Castle

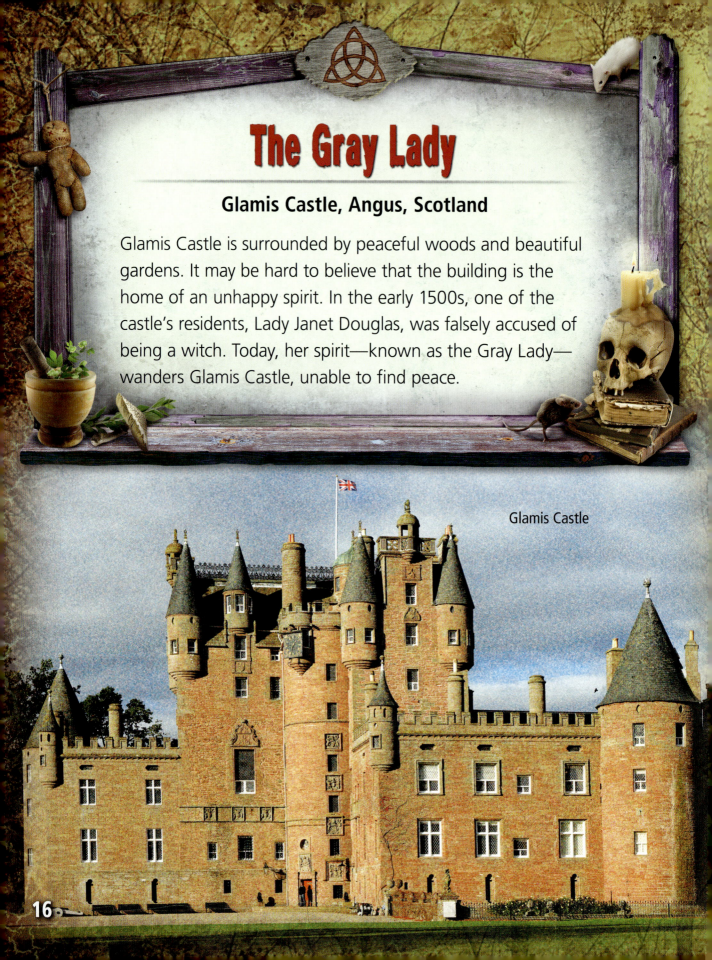

King James V of Scotland had always had a troubled relationship with members of the Douglas family, and he looked for ways to punish them. In 1537, he claimed that Lady Janet Douglas was a witch who planned to kill him with magical potions. The king ordered everyone living with Lady Janet in Glamis Castle to be arrested and tortured. One by one, her servants and family members were stretched on a **rack**. First, their wrists and ankles were tied to rollers on a wooden frame. Then, the rollers were cranked and the victim's limbs were slowly pulled apart. The pain was unbearable. Just to make the torture stop, Lady Janet's servants and family agreed to say she was a witch. Soon after, Lady Janet was burned at the stake.

King James V of Scotland

Today, visitors to Glamis Castle may catch a glimpse of Lady Janet . . . as a ghost. Some people say they have seen the Gray Lady in the castle's **chapel**, sitting in an empty seat that is saved just for her. She has also been seen in one of the castle's towers, looking as if she is tied to a stake and surrounded by flames.

A person being stretched on a rack

Many visitors who claim to have seen the Gray Lady say they felt an overwhelming sadness in her presence.

17

# The Fortuneteller

## Mother Shipton's Cave, Knaresborough, North Yorkshire, England

Along the River Nidd in northern England, there's a cave near a mysterious well that seems to turn objects to stone. According to legend, a witch named Mother Shipton was born in the cave in 1488. This beloved witch may have had very unusual powers and abilities.

Mother Shipton's Cave

It is said that Mother Shipton had a very large nose, and her back and legs were crooked. Because of her unusual appearance, local townspeople believed she was a witch. Yet, many thought that she was a very kind, gifted witch. She was known to use plants from the forest to make healing potions for the townsfolk.

Mother Shipton was also a poet who may have been able to predict the future. She wrote poems about "carriages without horses" hundreds of years before cars were invented. She described pictures that were "alive with movements free" before there were movies.

Mother Shipton

Today, many people visit the cave where Mother Shipton was born, as well as the nearby well. There's always a string of objects, such as shoes and teddy bears, hanging in the water. The water in the well appears to turn the objects to stone. However, there's a scientific explanation for this. What isn't explained is why many wishes made at the well are granted. That may be the work of Mother Shipton.

The water in the well near Mother Shipton's Cave contains lots of **minerals**. Objects left in the water become covered with the minerals, making them look like they've turned to stone.

teddy bears

Objects hanging at the well

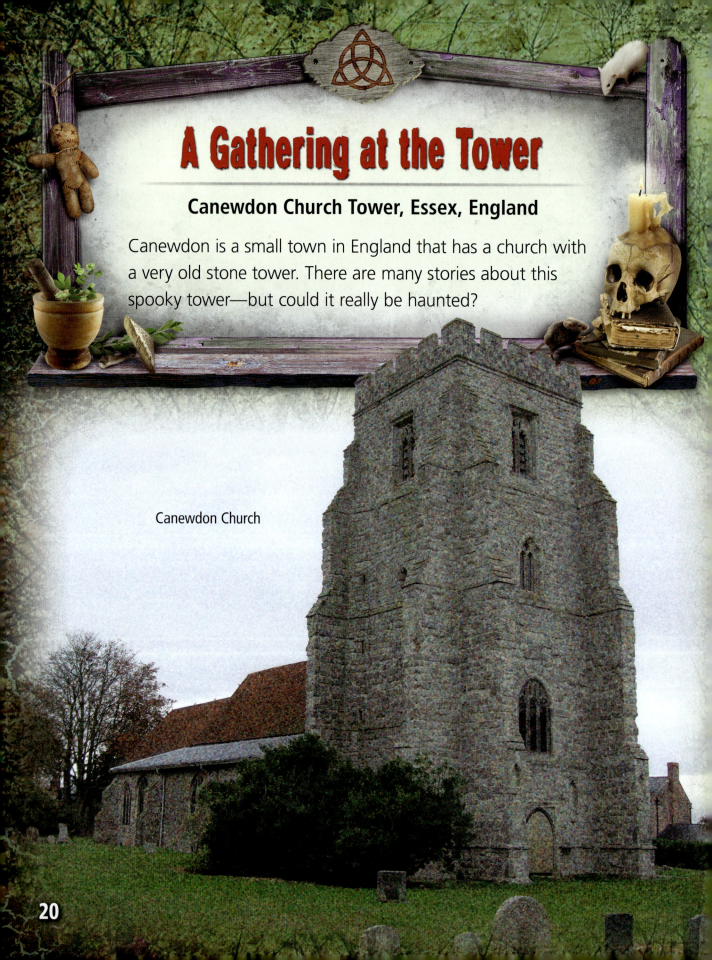

# A Gathering at the Tower

## Canewdon Church Tower, Essex, England

Canewdon is a small town in England that has a church with a very old stone tower. There are many stories about this spooky tower—but could it really be haunted?

Canewdon Church

It is said that there are always six witches living in Canewdon, and that when one dies, another takes his or her place. The Candewdon Church tower is popular with tourists looking to catch a glimpse of the witches or other **supernatural** beings. One legend says that anyone who walks around the tower at midnight will end up dancing with the witches.

Another legend says that walking around the tower 13 times makes a person invisible, but walking backwards around the tower three times makes a ghost appear. It's also believed that circling the tower on Halloween brings forth the devil, and going around it three times **counterclockwise** opens a **portal** to travel back in time. Could all the Canewdon legends be real?

Every Halloween, so many tourists come to the Canewdon Church tower to see witches, ghosts, and the devil that the police have to be called to control the huge crowds.

# The Killer Neighbor

## Bell Witch Farm and Cave, Robertson County, Tennessee

In Tennessee, there's a large farm near a gloomy cave. A deadly spirit sent by a witch once haunted the farm, and the witch now frightens visitors to the cave.

The reconstructed Bell farmhouse

In the early 1800s, John Bell and his family bought a farm in Tennessee. One day in 1817, they started hearing mysterious noises in their home, including loud banging on the walls, choking sounds, and heavy chains being dragged across the floor.

Soon, the haunting moved beyond just noises. John's daughter, Betsy, was scratched and hit by an unseen force. Sometimes John felt like he was being punched. Many people thought the hauntings were caused by a spirit sent by Kate Batts, a neighbor believed to be a witch.

After years of being tortured by the spirit, John fell seriously ill. One morning, a mysterious bottle of black liquid appeared next to his bed. His family worried that the spirit had given John poison, so they tested the liquid on a cat. The cat died soon after—and so did John. Whatever deadly game Kate had been playing, she finally won.

In 1821, just after John's death, the witch's spirit left the Bell farm. However, a local legend says she didn't go far. In a nearby cave, the spirit of Kate the Bell Witch is said to still roam.

Bell Witch Cave

Visitors to the Bell Witch Cave tell stories of being attacked by an invisible force. Some say they have been held on the ground and slapped.

# Quiet, Please!

## Tolbooth Tower, Pittenweem, Scotland

On the quiet coast of Scotland lies a fishing village called Pittenweem. Overlooking the sea stands the stone tower of the old Tolbooth, which was once used as a courtroom and a jail. Hundreds of years ago, this tower was where accused witches were held and tortured. Some say that the ghosts of those who died there cannot rest.

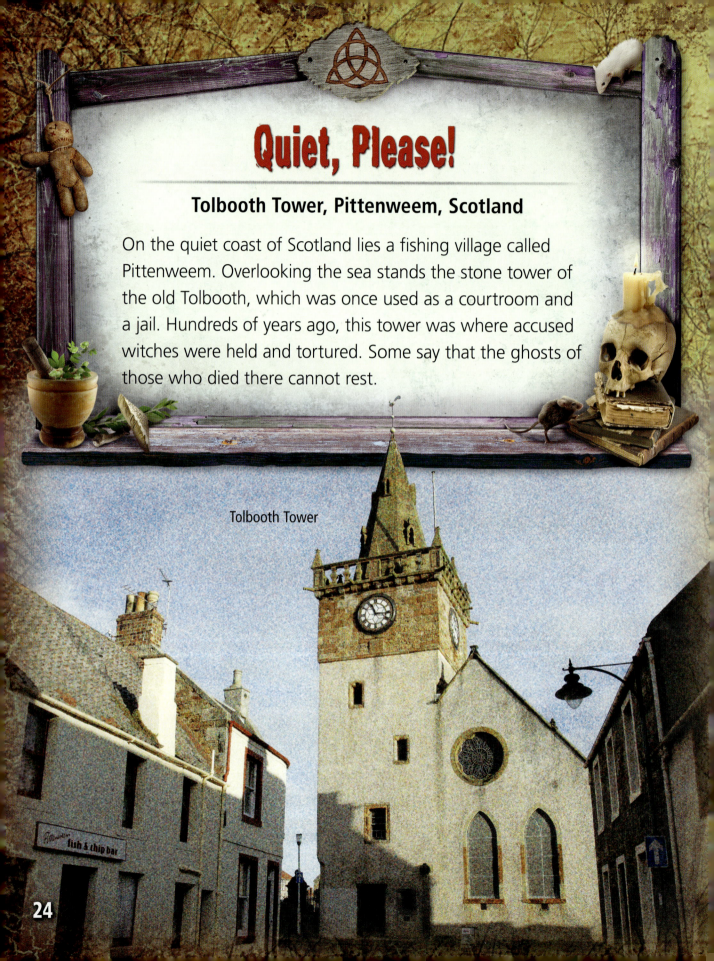

Tolbooth Tower

In 1705, after falling ill, Patrick Morton thought he had been cursed by his neighbors. One of his neighbors, Beatrix Laing, was accused of being a witch and jailed in the Tolbooth Tower. Her jailers kept her awake for days by pricking her with sharp objects. She was eventually released, but another accused witch, Janet Cornfoot, wasn't so lucky.

Janet escaped from her prison in the tower, but was caught by an angry **mob** of villagers. They tied her up, dragged her to the ocean's edge, beat her, and dunked her into the freezing water. Then the villagers piled heavy rocks on top of her. In case that didn't kill her, they rode a horse and cart over her body until they were certain she was dead.

An accused witch being dunked into water

Today, visitors can take tours of the tower. Unfortunately, the ghosts of the poor souls tortured there don't like the noisy tourists. One spirit was heard saying, "Too much talking!"

Some visitors to the tower have claimed to see a mysterious fog and floating **orbs** that appear then suddenly vanish.

# A Magical Festival

## Catemaco, Mexico

In southern Mexico, there is a small town, near a beautiful lake, where witchcraft is not feared. No one throws witches into dungeons, tortures them, or burns them at the stake. In fact, in Catemaco, a huge festival is held every year to celebrate witches and witchcraft.

The lake at Catemaco

On the first Friday of every March, a great festival begins at midnight. Witches—called *brujos* (BROO-hohs) in Spanish—gather in the town. On the first night, there is a ceremony with a burning **pentagram** at its center. There is **chanting** and dancing, and the devil is called upon.

A burning pentagram

The festival lasts for three days, and thousands of visitors come to watch and participate. Some festivalgoers look for good-luck spells or love potions. Others buy **amulets** for protection from harm and evil spirits. Witches tell fortunes and heal wounds with potions made from special plants and oils.

However, not all the magic performed at the festival is helpful, healing magic. Spells of revenge can be purchased to cast on an enemy. It is said there are brujos who will make a deal with the devil and send a curse of death!

Witchdoctors are very important in the area around Catemaco. There are even special kinds of witchdoctors, called *culebreros*, who heal snakebites.

# Witch Haunts

**Joshua Ward House**
**Salem, Massachusetts**

A cruel witch-killing sheriff haunts the site of his old home.

NORTH AMERICA

*Pacific Ocean*

*Atlantic Ocean*

**Bell Witch Farm and Cave**
**Robertson County, Tennessee**

A witch who once tormented her neighbor now attacks visitors to a cave.

**Festival of Witches**
**Catemaco, Mexio**

A festival is held every year to celebrate witchcraft.

**Rose Hall**
**St. James, Jamaica**

An evil plantation owner still keeps watch over her home.

SOUTH AMERICA

# Around the World

## Glamis Castle
**Angus, Scotland**

Lady Janet's ghost returned to her castle home after she was burned at the stake.

## Tolbooth Tower
**Pittenweem, Scotland**

The ghosts of accused witches want peace and quiet.

## Mother Shipton's Cave
**Knaresborough, North Yorkshire, England**

A kind, fortune-telling witch was born in a cave near a mysterious well.

## Canewdon Church Tower
**Essex, England**

Many people visit the tower to bring forth ghosts, witches, and the devil.

## Kyteler's Inn
**Kilkenny, Ireland**

An innkeeper escaped execution, but came back to her inn as a ghost.

## Moosham Castle
**Unternberg, Austria**

Witches who were tortured and killed in the castle dungeon never left.

## Lambi Dehar Mines
**Mussoorie, India**

A screaming witch and thousands of ghosts haunt abandoned mines.

Arctic Ocean

EUROPE

ASIA

AFRICA

Indian Ocean

AUSTRALIA

Southern Ocean

ANTARCTICA

# Glossary

**amulets** (AM-yuh-lets) small objects worn to protect people against evil

**beheaded** (bih-HED-id) had one's head chopped off

**bewitched** (bih-WICHT) placed under a spell by a witch

**branding** (BRAN-ding) burning with a red-hot iron as a form of torture

**chanting** (CHAN-ting) speaking or singing with no change in tone

**chapel** (CHAP-uhl) a building or room used for praying

**corpses** (KORP-siz) dead bodies

**counterclockwise** (*coun*-tur-CLOK-wyz) going in a circle opposite from the direction that the hands of a clock move

**curse** (KURSS) a spell that's intended to cause evil or harm

**dungeon** (DUHN-juhn) a dark prison cell, usually underground

**executed** (EK-suh-*kyoo*-tid) put to death

**legends** (LEJ-uhndz) stories handed down from the past that may be based on fact but are not always completely true

**limestone** (LIME-stohn) a rock that is used in building

**minerals** (MIN-ur-uhlz) the solid substances found in nature that make up rocks

**mob** (MOB) a large group of angry people

**mutilated** (MYOO-tih-*lay*-tid) cut off or destroyed necessary parts, such as limbs

**orbs** (AWRBZ) glowing spheres

**pentagram** (PEN-tuh-gram) a five-pointed, star-shaped figure sometimes associated with witchcraft

**portal** (PORE-tuhl) a door, gate, or entrance

**potions** (POH-shuhnz) mixtures of liquids used to make medicine, poisons, or drinks with magical powers

**rack** (RAK) a torture device on which a person's body is stretched in order to cause great pain

**spirit** (SPIHR-it) a supernatural creature, such as a ghost

**stake** (STAYK) a tall wooden post that a person who is being executed is tied to and then burned

**supernatural** (*soo*-pur-NACH-ur-uhl) something unusual that breaks the laws of nature

**terrorized** (TERR-ur-izd) produced fear by acts of violence

**tortured** (TORE-churd) caused great pain to someone in order to get them to confess to a crime

**trial** (TRYE-uhl) an examination of evidence in a court to determine if someone is guilty or innocent of a charge

**voodoo** (VOO-doo) a religion that includes some traditional African and Caribbean beliefs

**witchcraft** (WICH-kraft) the actions or magical powers of a witch

# Bibliography

**Levack, Brian P.** *The Witch-Hunt in Early Modern Europe.* New York: Routledge (2015).

**Schiff, Stacy.** *The Witches: Salem, 1692.* New York: Little, Brown and Company (2015).

# Read More

**Parvis, Sarah.** *Creepy Castles (Scary Places).* New York: Bearport (2008).

**Stern, Steven L.** *Cursed Grounds (Scary Places).* New York: Bearport (2011).

**Williams, Dinah.** *Spooky Cemeteries (Scary Places).* New York: Bearport (2008).

**Yolen, Jane, and Heidi Elisabet Yolen Stemple.** *The Salem Witch Trials: An Unsolved Mystery from History.* New York: Simon & Schuster (2004).

# Learn More Online

To learn more about witch haunts, visit
**www.bearportpublishing.com/ScaryPlaces**

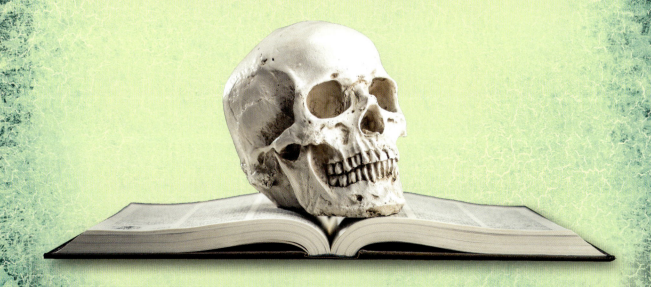

# Index

# About the Author

Heidi E.Y. Stemple is the author of books, poems, and short stories for young readers, several of which are about witches and ghosts. She lives on a big old farm in Massachusetts, home of the Salem witch trials.